Made in the USA
Middletown, DE
05 March 2022

62171475R00080